THE LIFE O

ALEXANDER
THE GREAT

By
Dr. Nicholas Saunders

School Specialty Publishing

Columbus, Ohio

THE CAST

Alexander III of Macedonia (Alexander the Great) *Alexander was born in July 356 B.C. at Pella to King Philip II and Queen Olympias. According to legend, the goddess Artemis attended his birth. Clever, tough, and resourceful, Alexander built the largest empire ever seen in the ancient world. It stretched from Greece to India. He died unexpectedly in Babylon in 323 B.C. at the age of 32.*

Philip II of Macedonia *Son of King Amyntas III and father to Alexander III, Philip became king in 359 B.C. He was a skilled and energetic soldier. His army reforms and string of victories transformed Macedonia into the most powerful state in Greece. He was assassinated at Aegae in the summer of 336 B.C.*

Olympias *She was King Alexander of Molossia's sister and a royal princess. She was also the wife of King Philip II of Macedonia and mother of Alexander III. Energetic and spiteful by nature, she was suspected of Philip's assassination. She was murdered during the chaotic wars of succession that followed Alexander's death.*

Hephaestion *Boyhood friend of Alexander who became his most intimate and life-long companion. Alexander appointed him Grand Vizier of the empire. He died unexpectedly at Ecbatana in October 324 B.C. A huge and expensive funeral was held for him in Babylon in 323 B.C., just weeks before Alexander's own death.*

Roxane *Bactrian princess and daughter of the Sogdian ruler Oxyartes. Alexander married her in 327 B.C. She gave Alexander his only legitimate heir, Alexander IV, but she and Alexander IV were murdered in Macedonia during the wars of succession that followed Alexander III's death.*

Darius III *King of the Persian empire. He ruled from 336 B.C.until defeated for a second time by Alexander at the Battle of Gaugamela in 331 B.C. He fled the battlefield but was murdered by the pretender king Bessus in 330 B.C.*

School Specialty.
Publishing

CONTENTS

SETTING THE SCENE

In 336 B.C., Alexander the Great (Alexander III) became king of Macedonia following the violent death of his father, King Philip II. He inherited a vast empire that included all of Greece, which he ruled from the city of Pella. Despite his young age of 20, the new king proved himself to be a skilled leader. In just 11 years, he and his army had conquered many countries, building the largest empire in the ancient world.

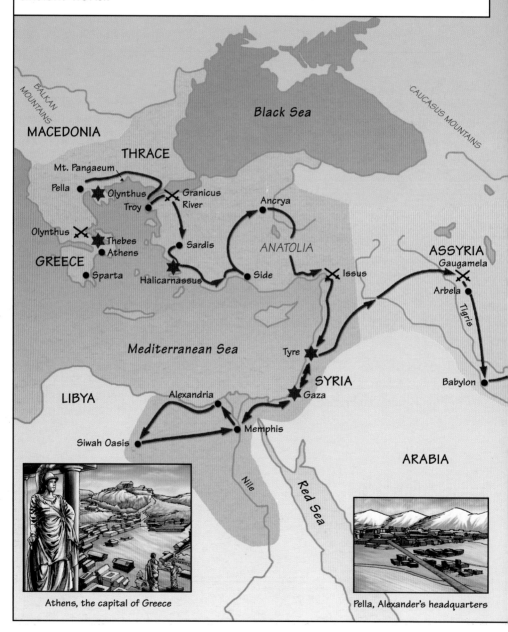

BALKAN MOUNTAINS

CAUCASUS MOUNTAINS

Black Sea

MACEDONIA

THRACE

Mt. Pangaeum

Pella

Olynthus

Troy

Granicus River

Ancrya

ANATOLIA

ASSYRIA

Gaugamela

Olynthus

Thebes

Athens

Sardis

GREECE

Sparta

Halicarnassus

Side

Issus

Arbela

Tigris

Mediterranean Sea

Tyre

SYRIA

Babylon

LIBYA

Alexandria

Gaza

Memphis

Siwah Oasis

Nile

Red Sea

ARABIA

Athens, the capital of Greece

Pella, Alexander's headquarters

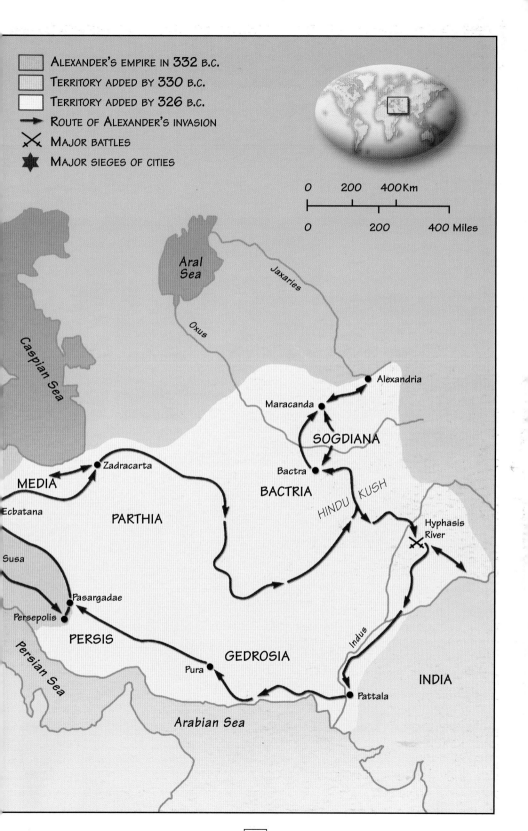

ALEXANDER'S EMPIRE IN **332** B.C.
TERRITORY ADDED BY **330** B.C.
TERRITORY ADDED BY **326** B.C.
ROUTE OF ALEXANDER'S INVASION
MAJOR BATTLES
MAJOR SIEGES OF CITIES

0   200   400 Km

0   200   400 Miles

Aral
Sea

Jaxartes

Oxus

Caspian Sea

Alexandria

Maracanda

SOGDIANA

Bactra

BACTRIA

HINDU KUSH

MEDIA

Zadracarta

Ecbatana

PARTHIA

Hyphasis
River

Susa

Pasargadae

Persepolis

PERSIS

Persian Sea

GEDROSIA

Pura

Indus

INDIA

Pattala

Arabian Sea

A YOUNG LEADER

Alexander's early years were adventurous. The goddess Artemis was said to have overseen his birth, which was thought to be a blessing. His intelligence and talent for hunting and fighting were quickly noticed. However, death and tragedy were also part of his youth.

On July 20, 356 B.C., Alexander was born in the royal palace at the Macedonian capital in Pella. Alexander's mother, Queen Olympias, presented the royal son to his father, King Philip.

King Philip's royal nobles gathered around to see the new baby who one day would become king of Macedonia.

At the same time as Alexander's birth, the Temple of Artemis in the great city of Ephesus was destroyed by a violent earthquake.

King Philip and his generals fought and celebrated at Pella after a military victory.

Under your leadership, we will conquer all of Greece and Persia!

Drink and eat, my generals! We have won another famous victory!

Oh, spirit of Dionysus, protect my son, Alexander. Make him lord of Asia!

Queen Olympias was devoted to the god Dionysus. She especially liked magic rituals that involved handling snakes.

In the palace at Pella, the young Alexander met Hephaestion for the first time. The two boys quickly became friends and developed a lifelong relationship.

Greetings, Hephaestion. I am Alexander, son of King Philip. Welcome to my father's city.

Thank you! I have heard so much about you. Perhaps we can be friends?

Alexander and Hephaestion hunted wild boar together. They learned skills they would use later when they hunted lions in Macedonia.

Watch out, Alexander! It may turn and charge your horse. Shoot it now!

Quick, Hephaestion! It's getting away! Throw your spear, and I'll shoot my arrow.

FAST FACT

In Alexander's time, there were no books. Scrolls of parchment, or papyrus, were used and rolled up to keep safe.

The Macedonian cavalry was made up of noblemen who could afford to own and take care of horses on their country estates. They trained constantly and were believed to be the best cavalry in the ancient world.

When Alexander was 12 years old, he watched his father's horse trainers struggle to tame an expensive wild stallion. Despite their strength and experience, the men were unable to control the horse, named *Bucephalus*.

Watch, father! I'll tame this wild stallion.

Careful, boy! He'll throw you right off.

Alexander noticed that Bucephalus was spooked by his own shadow. Alexander approached with the sun behind him and jumped on the horse's back and rode it across the plain.

Despite his youth, Alexander mastered Bucephalus. King Philip was so proud that he bought the horse for his son.

You did it, son! Macedonia is too small a kingdom for the likes of you. I'll buy Bucephalus, whatever the cost—the is horse is yours.

FAST FACT

Macedonian horses were small. They were not fitted with horseshoes, and stirrups had not yet been invented.

When Alexander was 16 years old, his father made him regent. This meant that Alexander was next-in-line to become king. Philip left on a campaign, leaving Alexander in charge.

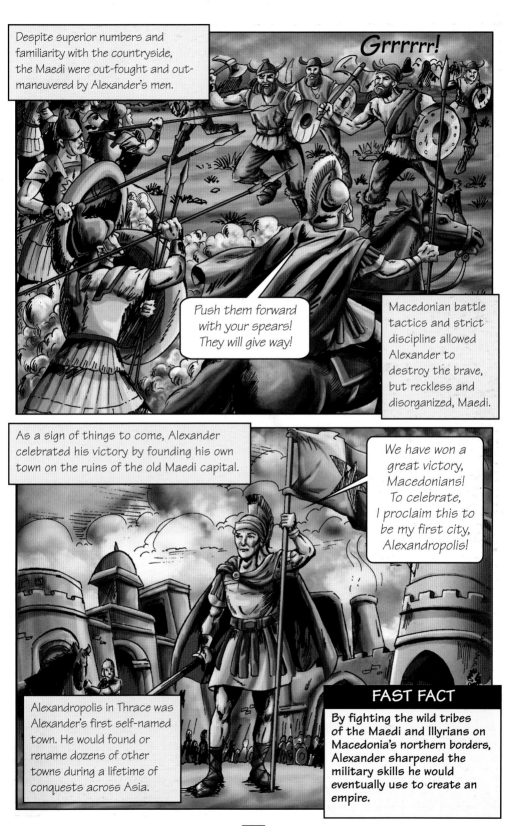

Despite superior numbers and familiarity with the countryside, the Maedi were out-fought and out-maneuvered by Alexander's men.

Grrrrr!

Push them forward with your spears! They will give way!

Macedonian battle tactics and strict discipline allowed Alexander to destroy the brave, but reckless and disorganized, Maedi.

As a sign of things to come, Alexander celebrated his victory by founding his own town on the ruins of the old Maedi capital.

We have won a great victory, Macedonians! To celebrate, I proclaim this to be my first city, Alexandropolis!

Alexandropolis in Thrace was Alexander's first self-named town. He would found or rename dozens of other towns during a lifetime of conquests across Asia.

FAST FACT

By fighting the wild tribes of the Maedi and Illyrians on Macedonia's northern borders, Alexander sharpened the military skills he would eventually use to create an empire.

Next, Alexander bravely faced the Theban warriors, called the Sacred Band, who vowed to fight to the death.

Stand firm, Thebans! We will defeat the Macedonians!

Macedonians, look! We shall fight the Thebans, the bravest of warriors!

In 338 B.C., the 18-year-old Alexander was given command of the elite Companion Cavalry. He led the troups to fight against Athens and their Theban allies at the Battle of Chaeronea in central Greece.

Flee, brothers. Alexander is upon us!

Charge! For Philip and Macedonia!

Charge!

Alexander's brilliant cavalry charge broke the Greek line and threw the Greeks into confusion. Many Greeks died as they tried to run from the battlefield.

The battle was hard. Alexander jumped off his horse and fought a bitter hand-to-hand struggle with the Thebans. Eventually, the Macedonians won the battle.

The Greeks and their allies suffered a terrible defeat. Philip congratulated his son and gave him the honor of returning the Athenian dead to Athens for burial.

King Philip, we, the Greeks, surrender to you and your mighty son.

Alexander, my son, your charge won the battle.

To honor the dead warriors, a giant funeral monument was erected. It was a great lion, made from white marble, that stood guard over the graves.

A NEW KING

Alexander's reputation grew during 336–331 B.C. He defeated Persian forces at the Battle of the Granicus River, besieged the great city of Halicarnassus, crushed Darius at Issus, and the captured the island city of Tyre. He captured Egypt, where he was made pharaoh, and built the city of Alexandria.

Stay here, Alexander. As father of the bride, I must enter the arena alone to be welcomed by the audience.

In the summer of 336 B.C., Philip entered the theater at Aegae with Alexander. Philip's daughter, Cleopatra, was celebrating her marriage to the king of Epirus.

Entering the arena alone, Philip was killed by his bodyguard, Pausanias.

Die, Philip! This is for the insults I have suffered and you have ignored.

Aaagh! Traitor! Traitor!

Quick! Don't let the assassin escape! He has killed the king!

Pausanias galloped away on a horse that had been left nearby. He was quickly chased by the other bodyguards.

Die, traitor!

Aaagh!

Before Pausanias could defend himself, the other bodyguards stabbed him to death.

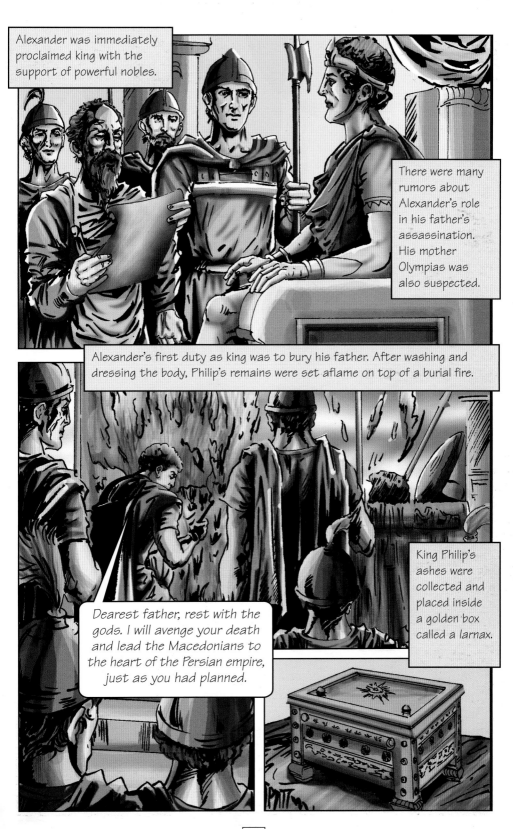

Alexander was immediately proclaimed king with the support of powerful nobles.

There were many rumors about Alexander's role in his father's assassination. His mother Olympias was also suspected.

Alexander's first duty as king was to bury his father. After washing and dressing the body, Philip's remains were set aflame on top of a burial fire.

Dearest father, rest with the gods. I will avenge your death and lead the Macedonians to the heart of the Persian empire, just as you had planned.

King Philip's ashes were collected and placed inside a golden box called a larnax.

In the spring of 334 B.C., the Macedonians invaded the Persian empire. Alexander was the first on shore.

Hurray! Alexander will conquer Persia!

I claim this land in the name of the gods!

Athena, goddess of war, I dedicate my armor to you.

Quick, Macedonians! Cross the river and charge the enemy.

Stand fast! The river will protect us.

Alexander dedicated his armor to Athena at her shrine near Troy. He took the armor of the hero Achilles in exchange.

In May, Alexander was victorious in his first battle against the Persians and their Greek allies, who were hired to fight with them. At the battle of the Granicus River, Alexander's life was saved by the Macedonian noble Cleitus the Black.

Alexander laid siege to the coastal city of Halicarnassus between August and September 334 B.C. He lost many men, but finally broke through the city's walls.

Attack the gate! It is giving way! We will rush them there!

In 333 B.C., in Phrygia, Alexander was challenged to undo the tangled Gordion knot by the prediction that whoever did so would conquer Asia. Alexander slashed the knot in half.

Alexander and his general, Ptolemy, stood in amazement before the huge burial mausoleum to King Mausolus.

Sir, Mausolus was a nobody. Your tomb will be even greater!

FAST FACT The Mausoleum at Halicarnassus stood about 150 feet tall and was built of limestone. At its summit was a statue of Mausolus driving a chariot. It is one of the Seven Wonders of the Ancient World.

THE BATTLE OF ISSUS

In November of 333 B.C., Alexander fought the Persian king Darius III on the coastal plains of Issus in Cilicia. Despite being outnumbered, the Macedonians defeated the Persians.

There is Darius! Charge and capture the tyrant King of Persia!

Alexander is coming! The city is lost!

Alexander besieged the island fortress city of Tyre between January and August 332 B.C. The Tyrians believed themselves safe behind their massive sheer walls and inflicted many casualties on the Macedonians.

Alexander won the battle when he charged furiously at Darius's chariot. The Persian king fled in panic, and the Macedonians captured his headquarters, treasures, and Darius's mother, Queen Sisygambis.

Alexander built a road from the shore to the island and stormed the city.
His men slaughtered many soldiers, crucified prisoners, and enslaved the survivors.

FAST FACT Alexander's determination to conquer Tyre and his inventive genius at building the causeway added awe and respect to his reputation as a brilliant general. It spread fear across Asia.

In November 332 B.C., Alexander and his army entered Egypt, defeating the small Persian garrison there. They were amazed by the huge pyramids at Giza and gazed in wonder at the mysterious stone face of the Sphinx.

What gods are these, Hephaestion? Surely no man could build such gigantic monuments!

Sir, I am told this sphinx was made for a pharaoh.

Hail, Alexander! We welcome you as our country's savior from the Persians. You are truly the new pharoah.

Alexander journeyed to the Egyptian capital at Memphis. While in Memphis, he was welcomed by the powerful Egyptian priesthood and made the new pharaoh.

Early in 331 B.C., Alexander's men rode across the Egyptian desert to reach the oracle temple of Ammon at Siwa. They were guided there by a flock of birds.

Quickly! Follow the birds. They are a sign from the gods and will guide us to Siwa.

Alexander and his men arrived safely at the Siwa oasis. Alexander walked to the oracle temple to hear what the oracle predicted for his future.

On April 7, 331 B.C., Alexander founded the city of Alexandria on Egypt's Mediterranean coast. He oversaw its building but never returned to see the work completed.

THE BATTLE OF GAUGAMELA

In 331 B.C., King Darius III and Alexander met again. Darius chose a wide, open plain near the village of Gaugamela for this battle. He led his army from Babylon and waited for Alexander. In September of 331 B.C., Alexander and 47,000 of his Macedonian troops arrived at Gaugamela.

The battle began between Alexander's cavalry and Darius's horsemen.

Darius used Indian elephants in the battle to scare Alexander's horses. Alexander's cavalry was smaller than the Persians, but they held off Darius's assaults.

Fight, horsemen, fight! We are losing too many men!

The horses are terrified by the great beasts, sir.

The Persian army had 200 war chariots with razor-sharp blades sticking out from the axles of the wheels. The chariots charged across the plain toward the Macedonian lines.

Use your arrows and spears to kill the chariot drivers!

When a Persian chariot driver was killed or injured, the Macedonian soldiers caught the horses and chariots. Trained war horses were great battle prizes.

Sir, Hephaestion has been wounded.

Alexander's closest friend, Hephaestion, was injured on the arm by a spear.

Doctors waited behind the battle lines to treat the injured.

Send my own doctor, Philip of Acarnania, to help him. Keep me updated!

The fighting continued for many hours. Alexander and his men fought their way closer and closer to Darius's camp.

Sir! Look! A gap has opened in the Persian line of defense!

Finally, the two leaders saw each other. Alexander did not hesitate; he led his men through the Persian ranks directly toward King Darius.

Alexander killed Darius's chariot driver. But before Alexander could attack Darius, Darius jumped from his chariot and ran from the battlefield, ending the battle.

In October 331 B.C., Alexander's army marched south. They entered the great city of Babylon through its magnificent Ishtar Gate.

We will enter Babylon through the Ishtar Gate and take control of the city.

Alexander and his men stood amazed at the great stepped temple that towered above the city of Babylon, honoring the god Marduk.

Mighty Marduk! Never before have I seen such a temple reaching to the sky!

As Babylon's new ruler, Alexander ordered the city's treasury to be taken with them.

Seize the treasury! All Persian gold belongs to me!

Alexander arrived at the sacred Persian capital of Persepolis in the spring of 330 B.C. He found a magnificent city containing another large treasury of gold and silver.

Another hoard of Persian treasure is now ours. I will use it to pay my soldiers.

In April, after a great banquet, Alexander set fire to the Great Palace.

May the gods be pleased! Let us sacrifice the Persian capital to the flames!

Alexander paid his respects to Cyrus the Great, the founder of the Persian empire, at his tomb at Pasargadae.

ALEXANDER IN INDIA

In the spring of 329 B.C., Alexander led his army across the snowy mountains of the Hindu Kush. He was heading for Bactria, chasing after the Persian king Bessus, who had declared himself Darius's successor. Alexander paid his older soldiers and sent them home.

Forward, Macedonians. We must capture Bessus, even if we follow him beyond the sky mountains.

Where are we heading? No man can cross these mountains!

Alexander's general, Ptolemy, captured Bessus, who was later murdered. Alexander crossed the great Oxus River and took the Sogdian city of Maracanda. He moved north, crossed the Jaxartes River, and founded Alexandria Eschate, which meant Alexandria the Furthest.

In the spring of 327 B.C., Alexander attacked the so-called indestructable fortress called *Sogdian Rock*. It belonged to the local ruler Oxyartes.

Forward, Macedonians! We must take this fortress!

After the capture of Sogdian Rock, Alexander married Oxyartes's daughter, the beautiful Bactrian princess Roxane. Although the alliance had political benefits, the marriage was a loving one, too.

Roxane, you shall be my queen and mother of my heir.

Alexander, I love you, too.

Late in 327 B.C., Alexander recrossed the Hindu Kush and led his army through the Khyber Pass and down to the lush plains below. His invasion of India had begun.

At last, we leave the cold mountains behind and welcome the heat of India. Here, there are new enemies to conquer.

In May 326 B.C., Alexander finally confronted the army of the Indian leader Porus. Alexander organized his Companion Cavalry and infantry to face the enemy.

The Macedonians saw for the first time the vast size of Porus's forces: 30,000 infantry, 4,000 cavalry, 1,000 war chariots, and 200 war elephants.

Quick! We must stop Porus's advance!

Look, Macedonians! The Indian army is like a sea of men!

Macedonians! Shields together and spears held high!

The Macedonians were astonished to see Raja Porus himself leading his massive ranks of armored war elephants into battle.

Sir, watch the enemy run. They are scared of your elephants!

We must be careful. Alexander has a fearsome reputation.

FAST FACT Indian elephants are smaller and more easily tamed than African ones. Two men sat on each elephant. One threw spears and shot arrows at their enemies, while the other controlled the animal.

To surprise Porus, Alexander took a large force 20 miles upstream and crossed a wide river. He planned to outflank the Indians and fight on a battlefield of his own choosing.

We must cross the river before Porus discovers our trick!

Cut and slash the elephants' legs! It is their weakest point!

Aaagh!

Alexander's strategy worked. He and his soldiers destroyed the Indian cavalry. Then, they attacked Porus's elephants and infantry. The Indians fought hard, but they were defeated.

Porus refused to surrender and fought bravely to the end. Alexander sent ambassadors to request his surrender, which Porus finally agreed to. Alexander made the raja an ally and allowed him to retain his kingdom.

I must stop Alexander. If he is killed, the Macedonians will be defeated.

Alexander's horse Bucephalus was mortally wounded during the battle. Alexander founded a city in the horse's honor, naming it *Bucephala*.

Bucephalus, my faithful horse since childhood. Now, you will gallop on the Elysian Fields.

THE FINAL YEARS

After defeating Porus, Alexander's army revolted when he ordered them to go further into India. Alexander nearly died from an Indian arrow, a disastrous desert crossing left tens of thousands dead, and the army revolted a second time at Opis. Alexander's dearest friend, Hephaestion, died in October 324 B.C. Alexander himself died just a few months later in June 323 B.C.

In June 326 B.C., Alexander marched the victorious army east to the Hyphasis river. Here, the army revolted. They had been fighting for eight years with no end in sight. Alexander decided he would return to Babylon.

Many of Alexander's soldiers were over 60 and had fought with King Philip. They now wanted to enjoy their lives, and they did not want to continue fighting for Alexander's personal glory.

Alexander led his army back to the Hydaspes river where his carpenters began building a fleet of ships that would transport them downriver to the Indian Ocean.

Let's make this a good ship that will take us safely home.

In early 325 B.C., Alexander attacked a town belonging to the Malli tribe. He was trapped and nearly killed. He eventually recovered from his wounds.

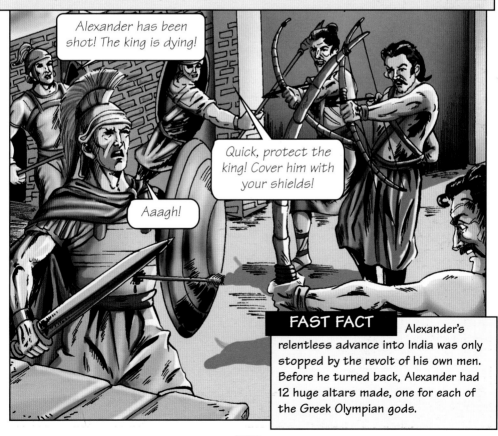

Alexander has been shot! The king is dying!

Quick, protect the king! Cover him with your shields!

Aaagh!

FAST FACT Alexander's relentless advance into India was only stopped by the revolt of his own men. Before he turned back, Alexander had 12 huge altars made, one for each of the Greek Olympian gods.

From November 326 until August 325 B.C., Alexander and his fleet sailed down the Hydaspes and Indus rivers until they reached Pattala. From here, Alexander began crossing the Gedrosian desert. His admiral, Nearchus, sailed to the Indian Ocean.

Alexander marched across the Gedrosian desert for 60 days. It was so hot that Alexander and his army had to march at night. Supplies failed to appear, and water and food ran dangerously low.

Thousands of soldiers, women, and children died of thirst and had to be left behind unburied. By the time Alexander emerged from the desert, he had lost about 60,000 lives of the original 85,000. It was the biggest disaster of his life.

Leave me, wife. I cannot go on. Save yourself and our child.

Let the desert drink this! If my army cannot drink, neither shall I.

Sir, you must drink. We only have a little water left!

Alexander shared the hardships of the desert march. He walked his horse and refused to drink water when so many others could not.

In the autumn of 324 B.C., Alexander marched his army into the Zagros mountains to the city of Ecbatana. Here, he celebrated ten years of victories in Asia with magnificent athletic games, music, and plays for his army.

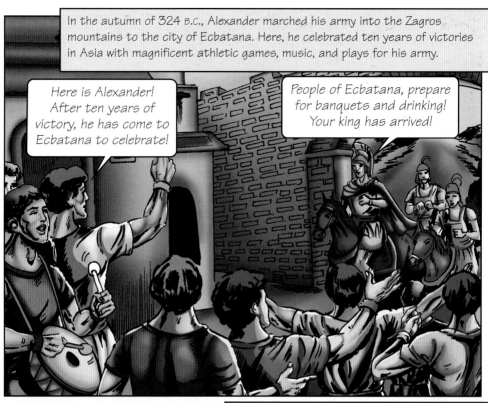

Here is Alexander! After ten years of victory, he has come to Ecbatana to celebrate!

People of Ecbatana, prepare for banquets and drinking! Your king has arrived!

In October, Hephaestion was taken ill during a banquet and died. Alexander was heartbroken.

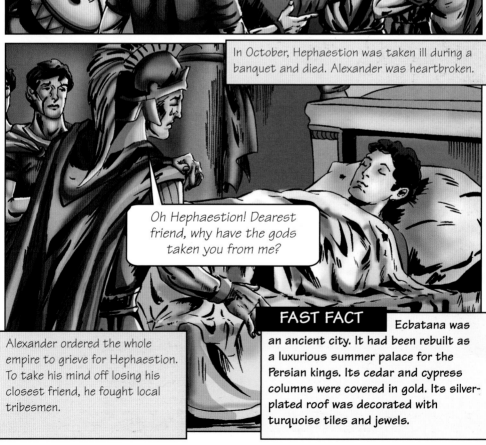

Oh Hephaestion! Dearest friend, why have the gods taken you from me?

Alexander ordered the whole empire to grieve for Hephaestion. To take his mind off losing his closest friend, he fought local tribesmen.

FAST FACT

Ecbatana was an ancient city. It had been rebuilt as a luxurious summer palace for the Persian kings. Its cedar and cypress columns were covered in gold. Its silver-plated roof was decorated with turquoise tiles and jewels.

Alexander returned to Babylon in early 323 B.C. to bury his friend and to plan for an invasion of Arabia. Banquets, paid for from the riches of Asia, were held almost every night.

On his deathbed, Alexander called his generals and friends to him. He gave his royal signet ring to Perdiccas, the empire's Grand Vizier, but he added that the empire would go to the strongest man.

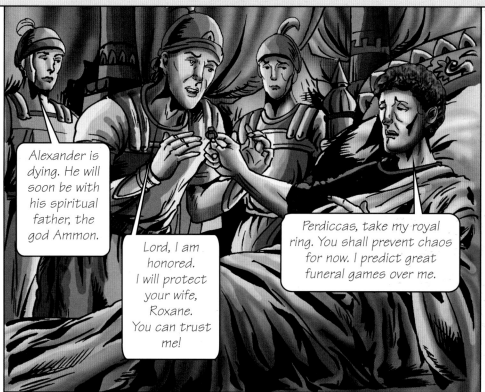

Alexander is dying. He will soon be with his spiritual father, the god Ammon.

Lord, I am honored. I will protect your wife, Roxane. You can trust me!

Perdiccas, take my royal ring. You shall prevent chaos for now. I predict great funeral games over me.

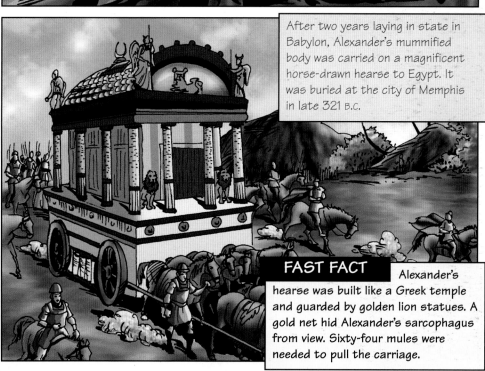

After two years laying in state in Babylon, Alexander's mummified body was carried on a magnificent horse-drawn hearse to Egypt. It was buried at the city of Memphis in late 321 B.C.

FAST FACT Alexander's hearse was built like a Greek temple and guarded by golden lion statues. A gold net hid Alexander's sarcophagus from view. Sixty-four mules were needed to pull the carriage.

Alexander's short but spectacular life was full of adventure. He fought many battles over a large area and was involved in numerous plots and murders. This timeline and fast fact section fills in some of the gaps in Alexander's extraordinary life.

July 20, 356 B.C.: *Alexander's birth.*

343: *Alexander is taught by Aristotle at Mieza.*

340–339: *Alexander is named regent at Pella during Philip's absence.*

336: *Philip is assassinated at Aegae; Alexander becomes king as Alexander III.*

335: *Alexander fights the the Illyrians and the Triballi tribe in Thrace.*

334: *Alexander takes command of the invasion of Persia and crosses into Asia.*

May 334: *Battle of the River Granicus.*

September 334: *Alexander takes Halicarnassus.*

Spring 333: *Alexander campaigns in Phrygia and cuts the Gordion knot.*

November 333: *Alexander fights and defeats the Persians at the Battle of Issus.*

January-August 332: *Siege and eventual destruction of Tyre.*

November 332: *Alexander enters Egypt and is named pharaoh.*

January–March 331: *Alexander visits Siwa Oasis and is welcomed as the "Son of Ammon." Alexander founds Alexandria on Egypt's Mediterranean coast.*

October 1, 331: *Alexander defeats the Persians at the Battle of Gaugamela.*

October–December 331: *Alexander marches south to Babylon, Susa, and Persepolis.*

May 330: *Alexander burns the great palace at Persepolis.*

Spring 329: *Alexander crosses the Hindu Kush to Bactra.*

Summer 329: *Capture and execution of Bessus.*

November 328: *Alexander murders Cleitus the Black at Maracanda.*

Spring 327: *Capture of Sogdian Rock. Alexander marries Roxane.*

Winter 327: *Alexander recrosses the Hindu Kush and invades India.*

May 326: *Alexander defeats the Indian raja Porus at the Battle of the Hydaspes.*

June 326: *Macedonian army revolts and Alexander decides to return to Babylon.*

Spring 325: *Alexander wounded while assaulting a town of the Malli tribe.*

September–October 325: *March through the Gedrosian desert.*

April 234: *Mass weddings of Macedonians and Persian women at Susa.*

June 324: *Macedonian army mutinies at Opis; Alexander reconciles them.*

October 324: *Alexander's close friend Hephaestion dies in Ecbatana.*

June 11, 323: *Alexander dies in Babylon at the age of 33.*

1. *The kingdom of Macedonia in northern Greece was composed of thirteen regions. Macedonians were considered rough and unsophisticated by the Greeks of Athens and Thebes.*

2. *Alexander's father, King Philip II, made Macedonia into a powerful imperial state. He set the stage for Alexander by conquering the southern Greek city-states and ruling them in his role as hegemon (leader) of the League of Corinth.*

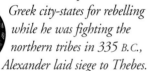

3. *Determined to punish the Greek city-states for rebelling while he was fighting the northern tribes in 335 B.C., Alexander laid siege to Thebes. After his victory, he destroyed the city completely as a warning to others.*

4. *Alexander's most dangerous enemy in the early years of the invasion of Asia was the mercenary Greek general Memnon. Memnon fought against the Macedonians until his death in 333 B.C.*

5. *In 334 B.C., after his successful siege of Halicarnassus, Alexander adopted the city's former queen, Ada, as his honorary mother. He appointed her governor of the whole region of Caria and left his general Ptolemy with her for a year.*

6. *In November and December 331 B.C.,*

Alexander stormed the mountainous lands of the Uxii, breaking through the Persian Gates. He then marched on Persepolis.

7. *One of Alexander's most famous victories was his 326 B.C. capture of the almost inaccessible Rock of Aornus in what is today northern Pakistan.*

8. *In July 325 B.C., Alexander's former treasurer, Harpalus, arrived in Athens with a vast amount of gold and silver he had stolen from Alexander while Alexander was in India.*

9. *In the months before his own death, Alexander planned for the invasion of Arabia by building a huge fleet of ships and converting Babylon into a strong port city.*

10. *Alexander had Hephaestion's body mummified at Ecbatana. Alexander cremated Hephaestion's remains at a huge funeral in Babylon in the summer of 323 B.C., just weeks before he himself died.*

11. *Many murder conspiracies circulated in the weeks and months after Alexander's death. Some believed that Alexander's own cup bearer, Iolaus, poisoned Alexander's wine, while others believed a conspiracy of the top generals was a possibility.*

12. *After Alexander's death, his generals fought a bitter struggle for the succession. In a daring battle, Ptolemy stole Alexander's embalmed body from Damascus in 321 B.C. and buried it at Memphis in Egypt. Alexander's body was later reburied in Alexandria.*

GLOSSARY

Aegae: *Original Macedonian capital before Pella was built. It became the sacred burial ground of the Macedonian kings. King Philip II, Alexander's father, was murdered in its theater.*

Alexandria: *Officially* Alexandria-by-Egypt, *the city was founded by Alexander in 331 B.C. at the western extreme of the Nile Delta. It became the largest and most successful of the many Alexandrias that Alexander created.*

Ammon: *Greek version of the Egyptian god Amun, sometimes combined with Zeus, king of the Olympian gods in Greece.*

Aristotle: *Famous Greek philosopher (384–322 B.C.) whose father had been the royal doctor to King Philip's father, Amyntas III. Alexander sent Aristotle specimens of plants and animals from his Asian campaigns and travels.*

Babylon: *Great city built on the banks of the rivers Tigris and Euphrates in Mesopotamia. It was surrounded by double walls and featured eight gates. It was dedicated to the local god, Marduk. Babylon was where Alexander died on June 10, 323 B.C.*

Bessus: *He murdered his relative King Darius, was captured by Ptolemy, and executed by Alexander in 329 B.C.*

Chaeronea: *Famous battle in 338 B.C. between the Macedonians, led by Philip and Alexander, and an alliance of Greek cities, led by Athens and Thebes. Notable for ending the independence of the Greek city-states.*

Chiliarchy: *A unit of 1,000 men in the Macedonian army.*

Cleitus the Black: *Macedonian nobleman who saved Alexander's life at the Battle of the Granicus. Alexander murdered him during a drunken fight in 328 B.C.*

Cyrus the Great: *Founder of the Persian empire (559–530 B.C.) who died fighting to expand his realm near the Caspian Sea. He was buried at Pasargadae, near Persepolis.*

Darius III: *Persian king who confronted Alexander. He assassinated the previous king, Artaxerxes IV, to become king. He is often regarded as weak in his dealings with Alexander.*

Dionysus: *Greek god of wine, excess, and disguise. Alexander and his mother Olympias were faithful followers of Dionysus. Dionysus' mythical adventures in India inspired Alexander to campaign there, as well.*

Gordion knot: *An intricate knot that was tied to the funeral hearse of the mythical King Gordius at the Phrygian capital of Gordium. It was said that anyone who could untie it would rule Asia. Alexander slashed it with his sword, and the prediction was fulfilled.*

Hephaestion: *Alexander's childhood friend, whose friendship lasted his whole life. The two men were compared to Homer's heroes, Achilles and Patroclus.*

Hoplites: *Greek infantrymen who carried round shields and spears.*

Marduk: *Main god of the Babylonians whose great temple dominated the city's skyline.*

Nearchus: *Born in Crete, Nearchus was a childhood friend of Alexander and later became Admiral of the Fleet in the voyage to the Indian Ocean.*

Olympias: *Alexander's mother and a princess of the neighboring kingdom, Molossia. She was cruel, spiteful, and may have been behind the assassination of Alexander's father, King Philip II.*

Parmenion: *Senior general of the Macedonian army under King Philip II and Alexander. He was murdered after Alexander had Parmenion's eldest son, Philotas, killed for treason.*

Pella: *New Macedonian capital built in the 5th century B.C. It became a sophisticated imperial capital under King Philip II.*

Persepolis: *Ceremonial capital of the Persian empire. It was built by King Darius I and his son, Xerxes. It was destroyed by fire at Alexander's command in 330 B.C.*

Phalanx: *The line of infantry arranged for battle.*

Philip II: *Alexander's father who transformed Macedonia from a weak region into a strong military state through army reforms and a string of military victories.*

Porus: *Fearless raja of the Punjab region in India. He fought Alexander at the Hydaspes River and became, after his defeat, an ally of the Macedonians.*

Ptolemy: *Macedonian noble and childhood friend of Alexander who accompanied him across Asia. He was rewarded for his loyalty and fighting skill by being made a Marshal of the Empire. After Alexander's death, he became king of Egypt.*

Roxane: *Bactrian princess who became Alexander's wife after his victory at Sogdian Rock. She gave Alexander his only legitimate heir, Alexander IV.*

Sacred Band: *A group of 300 Theban warriors formed into 150 pairs that vowed to fight to the death at the Battle of Chaeronea against the Macedonians. They are honored by a marble lion statue that still stands.*

Sarissa: *A long infantry spear invented by King Philip, and a deadly weapon in the hands of well-trained army units. It was 16 feet long and was held in both hands.*

Satrap: *Greek version of the Persian word that meant* provincial governor.

Siwa: *Large desert oasis in Egypt and home to the sacred oracle of the god Ammon. Alexander consulted it in 332–331 B.C. From then on, he regarded himself as the divine son of Ammon.*

Susa: *The administrative capital of the Persian empire, where records were kept in cuneiform script cut into sun-dried clay tablets. Alexander held his mass wedding between Macedonians and Persians here in 324 B.C.*

INDEX